Carol Rumens is twenty-eight and lives in Old Coulsdon with
her husband and two small daughters. She was
educated at convents and (briefly) at London University, and
works as a freelance arts reviewer. She is interested
in most forms of liberation, particularly women's and children's,
which is reflected strongly in some of her poetry.

Carol Rumens

A Strange Girl in Bright Colours

QUARTET BOOKS   LONDON

First published in Great Britain
by Quartet Books Limited 1973
27 Goodge Street, London WIP IFD

Copyright © 1973 by Carol Rumens

ISBN 0 704 33026 1

Printed in Great Britain by Acorn Litho Services Ltd,
Feltham, Middlesex

Typesetting by Bedford Typesetters Ltd, Bedford

Designed by Gerald Cinamon

A Strange Girl
in Bright Colours

Birth

Prologue

Quietly the sky measures
the lengthening days. Her blue

pallor is blotted with cloud messages
– the indecipherable

desires of chain-footed february.
Out of the garden's squalor

breathlessly climbing,
the trees enmesh themselves

in buds black as barbs.
The sky says nothing

about hope or rewards.
Newness is terrifying.

Now the birds resume
their tinselling cries

that dismiss starvation and snow.
There are eyes, flower-small,

opening in the hedges,
shedding a strange light.

Stones have been shifted.
A memory of love,

an impossibility,
pecks at barrenness.

O lonely month
with your hard frosts and soft tears,

you tap and won't be silenced.
You demand action

– a deed, a commitment,
a wound to be root-filled.

Like the shiver of catkins
I hang these words upon you.

Bon Voyage

I was unloaded from the clouds
into this white bed by the white window.
Bored and untried, I long to embark.
The waves sing, my pulse rate has dropped to a calm,
my blood pressure is ridiculously normal,
yet it's unsafe here. Why is nothing happening?
Hour after hour the sun gushes boiling water
into the white harbour of the room.
I don't rock. I am stiff with pillows
forcing my eyes into the sun's down-pour;
in my frost-starched night-gown a dead
white hulk hung out to dry,
touched once by antiseptic fingers that speared
my bag of waters this morning – only this morning?
It is two o'clock, yes, they are still drizzling,
leaking like slow snow.
I look at beautiful girls in magazines
– brown angels from flat impossible summer-times –
rows of them, like cut-out dolls on the sand,
and wait for thunder, the other heart-beat
of my god-like engine. I imagine it, I ache for it.
I am no relation to these strangers
– their flesh is a lie, their sands too constant – I
am leaving to-night, earlier if possible.

Pulsing in its white hood like a fist,
my light defies the staff-nurse and her peep-hole.

My fruit, my purse, my filled glass, gather their glitters
all night and touch my eyes concernedly.
It is so late it is tomorrow. My fate
waits for news of me in a different room,
another country, nude, vast and brilliant,
with its needles, tubes and dishes.
Is it for me they gleam attentiveness,
and listen for the rumble of one more trolley?
They are mistaken. I should not be here at all.
The doctors are planning to send me home,
my papers lost, my body a nameless imposter.
The clouds are so black now I can't see them.
What are they doing, what are these foot-steps creaking
the decks of my misery?
They are outward-bound, I think they are hurrying
sailors remembering girls' bodies
in the lash of the sea.
Hearing human voices, the stars excite.
And at last you wrench me
while I sleep, like a bell.
The red plug leaps from me.
I spring into the night, my engines roaring.

A Death

The night after the birth
moves over me like a black lid.

It shuts on my strange belly,
and my legs, bone-thin as fossils.

I can't move, portents lurk in my muscles.
My vagina, clamped by seven slit stitches

across her enormous wound,
seeps the red dews in silence.

Staunch as a matron, sleep steps up to see
whose bed-light is still on,

whose pre-natal magazines still nervously mutter.
She stops at my obsolete body.

She is stronger than pethidine.
Embalming fluid fills her needle.

I sink until morning
when the voice streams from the cradle like shifting ice,

when a new age flickering in white wraps
shows the cold its wrung

fistful of planets, tipping the world with a cry,
and I rise like Lazarus, old and terrified.

Afterwards

FOR KELSEY, AGED FIVE

Red egg, made lean with tunnelling
my valleys, your scalp mapped blue
with a blood-stream already ancient,

and your voice, so unprecedented,
ringing like an alarm
in a blitz of cold vibrations,

you broke into my consciousness
– sweet dawn after crossing a world
– my Antipodean sun-rise.

This hand, dismissing its tremor,
touched your own waxy star.
Pulses fused again. Time stopped.

From later, more complex birthdays
we have travelled, and debased
the language of fingers and mouths.

Now we touch only through tears,
or at night, in dark and pain.
My kisses remorseful, too hot,

choke the clear breath of your dream
like a strangler's hesitant shadow.
You prepare your mind for my funeral.

Sonnet

I like the baby's song, raw and glad,
as we ride home in the bus, in the year's gut-end;
an ambulance shrieks, the sun is nobody's friend,
but the small voice sings and sings of love well-starred.

Though it cried, will cry again, and, some time, die,
it does not ask to be married or insured.
These rough-haired vowels my children also purred,
are whole and ample worlds. Too soon they'll try

the nervier pitch, the riddle of consonants
which now these grown-ups sift, or else have lost
in speechless doubt. Chainsmoking, moping past
waste-heaps of passion, dregs of indifference,

no lowly ancestor can sing them home.
They travel like poison to the child's sweet tongue.

Menopause

No pains, no mid-wife now;
this is the dud season
set between extremes,
when the travel-agent prints

red skies, gold skins
on the flat eye of the future.
It shuts. A woman mounts
her ageing escalator,

treading the rutted years
for music, like a stylus.
She catches, catches.
Her body glides by

on a pitiless turn-table.
The light drops from her hands
to another latitude where
thin girls laugh

in the fumey slip-stream,
their lives blowing outward.
This way, please, this way.
Here is a wooden cold,

a night unfit for journeys,
a night for turning home.
It is the twelfth month.
No baby cries.

Concern

Questions for Advent

Christmas. How can it be received?
An exorbitant gift,
it imposes itself upon an ungrateful season.

The multi-stars of snow,
coloured bells, fat candles,
pulse in the black air.

They are delectable fakes.
Blow on them, watch them melt.
Rub out the last drop.

How else can you breathe
among such excess, such metals
pumping and stamping, such clatter of tills?

How can you listen for a cry
when the carpenter's baby
is jamming the production lines

with a billion plastic duplicates,
or feel the heart-beat of
a love governed by arithmetic,

all bank-statements and rows of x's?
Even the innocent fir-tree
so entrancing now, in a month

will be stripped and dismissed.
And the pallid, original child, for all his
struggling giftedness,

will also come to a bad end,
leaving last desperate promises,
indecipherable and locked.

Christmas Greetings

Fog thickens on the rose-bush. The moon eyes
of slowed cars grope homewards.
                                    Don't despair.
The old romanticisms sound real tonight
– a string quartet gesturing ultimatums –
on the other channel the blaze of war
is sterilised in twenty-inch black-and-white,
and if a censored scream escapes, turn off.
Through fragile walls my neighbour's child coughs
one cough for hours between the ads and silence.
Our local mad-woman calls out for her husband;
her porch-light frying the grey air gold, she craves
home-comings, visitors, incessant chat
to radiate her mind's iced rooms.
                                    Don't listen.
In stiff dark copses now the multi-mouthed
holly broadcasts weather hard as death.
Don't worry. All the tills are wide awake.
God smiles from these Caesar-headed metals.
Our country's peaceful, though it has its poor
– scar-faced behind grey windows. Don't touch them.
The electrified manger bleeps from its new wrapper.

Superstore

CHRISTMAS, 1969

This is the factory that makes the master-race;
the place where the dead are sold, fully-processed,
and the starving swing on meat-hooks or drown in vats.

So, madam, take your choice
from these gutted scraps, these eyeless hunks
in their deep snow-shelvings,

this terrace of ripe-bellied jars,
this marble plateau stained
by fresh garbage of amputations,

beyond the citrus shores, the steep nut-beaches.
Dip your white fingers anywhere you please;
rub, thumb, select, discard

for your larder of gilded shrunken-heads.
This is the grist of despair
guaranteed, madam, to pack

a power-house of protein, contract
the first pulse of the master-heart,
and to gird an entire cell-structure

– bones like rocks, hair like branches,
eyes that see in the dark,
blood as dark as burning raisins.

How much, how much forgetfulness,
rich as pudding dough,
do you need to out-eat guilt?

We will sell you the lot, we have everything.
Our conveyor-strips ceaselessly slide.
This is the exit, here is the sky

carved from a nerveless blaze
where snow-crystals span their beaded
prayer-wheels over and over

the tunnel of the wind-iced street,
and the throats of the charity tins
cough on cold nickel, your hasty apologies.

Palaeolithic Incident

Wolves from the wolf-red cave,
and the sabre-toothed tiger
that prints the Mendip mud
with barbed soles, are moving.

The gorge drops her green
fogs like a witch-curse.
High on the falls of scree,
human feet

dart to where the trees thin
on distanceless rock
– ten anxious knuckles
that have lost their ape-grip, their

old steady rhythms
under the irretrievable
assurance of a tail.
Balked now by cold blades,

white quartz, black basalt,
the cave-man flattens.
His fingers scrape upward
for the scarred wet lips of owl holes

and momentary moss.
The first dews lightly touch
the leaves of the valley. He slips,
slips faster as rocks spin with elms,

pivots, and hangs magical
from a skein of dead tree.
Above him are grasslands, sky
and the small lamps of strawberries.

He will worship them with bites
whole off the stalk, will lie flat
and breathe levelly again.
One tug, and the plateau will be his.

He leaps from his dream, but the sky
plunges backwards, and he
knows that the tiger is standing
below, and he is falling.

Epilogue

Philanthropist and Poet
can't raze Auschwitz or the slums
though they build palace.
Care for the wounded won't deter
attacking armies,
and poet's artistry transforms
only his mental chaos.

Good men are devoted
to the dumb needs of the oppressed,
mercifully dealing
with all their patent ill-effects;
they do not dream
to treat the incurable cause, the ty
-rant's appalling fever.

And poets, though they see
the whole complexity of wrong,
do not chastise it;
their technique is only words
that make the worst
tolerable on paper and in the minds;
the killer still keeps killing.

Lost Things

Red undersides pulsing,
mouth opening, opening on naked air,
he sits about in the astonishment of his change
– tiny transparent frog –
half-tail'd still, and quick to return to the water,
his breast-stroke delicate, perfect;
but surfacing later, more boldly,
and, when nobody's watching,
suddenly leaping out to a lost life
somewhere in our back-garden, street, city.
Shrivelled by towering stone,
foot-snap or black squeeze of tyre,
he is meaningless in death, his seven weeks
of intricate life dulled to a clumsy joke.
I must not pity him. Let him become
as distant to me as newsreel refugees
poking about in small bowls, blind to the cameras.
They are all nature's expendables, a common clock-work
undone in seconds. To search
for soul or self, god-spark in every life,
is the last human myth.
The eye that counted hairs and the fall of sparrows
fails, is not even I, but a million i's,
leaping at dreams, dying in endless hunger.

Love

Biafrans

She still has her woman's body;
she drags its empty skin
step by step from the well of cynicism.

Her youngest child at her hip
lurches with closed eyes,
his life between her toes like the dust of wheat.

She carries him all day
back through the starved field of child-birth,
back to the first hunger of her cervix.

She returns him to the shadows'
falling bayonets.
The night swells like oedema, like a womb,

and a man's curses smother her; she's
his lost mirage. Her mouth in his, he cries,
and the bones of her pelvis fill his belly like meat.

From a Diary

Dear one, the week
slowly steps towards you. I'm frightened.
Fine mornings turn to rain by noon. Spring comes.
My eyes cloud with superfluous scenery
where images of you hustle and fade.
I sit by the telephone. The room darkens
into a featureless grief, and it is night.

The liberation of dreams
brings you back; we close upon a breath.
Peace creeps into the space between two skins.
Waking, my hands shake even to unseal
the vacant envelope, the far-travelled lie.
Merely to catch your glance across drinks and smiles
and murmured riddles about the weather, could kill.

Time and its slow rhythms
somehow sustain me; the transparent days
that pass like dancers carry me towards perfection.
They cannot reveal that the dance has no denouement,
how soon and bitterly each scene must be stripped.
Spring shakes the throats of the flowers. Winter watches.
The next act is unimaginable.

Night Song

A day of footloose sweetness, disenchanted
already, it begins to travel on.
The free can't keep from their double-locked apartments.
The city's watch-dogs can't detain the sun.

Outlawed, I gather up the words we dropped,
strain faded smiles from bottles left half-drunk
– garbage of memories cleansed, assembled, loved,
to challenge this city's boredom, this room's dark.

Though time's barbed wall divides our continents,
wired to my desperate hunger, you return,
melting its shadows. Now the city lights
rise like the sun. Dream-trapped all night, we burn.

New Addington

A New Addington Anthology

DISTINCTIONS

The green hill-spine bends
to the new development
where graduates raise tulips and two
denim'd kids apiece
in stucco semis; their
Conde Nast living-areas in glass cases swarm
along the poppy-field kept
by a rustic whim, begin
to claw that gravelly scoop
borrowed from the hill
and leased to artists all last summer. Strange
happenings of smoke-bombs, clowns,
masques and kinetic painting
brought down the T.V. cameras and the odd
police-car, light buzzing, a throttle of rage
before the sight-seers revved and tutted away
up the dirt road. I
walked it every night,
padding on secretive soles the miles between
July poetry readings in fierce sun-light
and the enclosed Blues of late September
under a skull of rain.
I came and listened, crouching, uneasy.
I didn't belong
to either sect whose sparse lords balefully glared
at each other across the sandy floor
as night fell. The poppies dripped away.

Taking their bits of poems in plastic bags
and flower'd vans full of old mattresses,
pale girls and boys pitched camp.
The residents lowered their blinds,
smiled, and turned the switch marked apathy.
Again I climbed the hill
to where the old estate in scabby mounds
of rented concrete hangs;
– it has no artistry, no wiles
but those of subsistence.
Its girls, with sober head-scarves and great prams,
shove for their lives.

One Street Beyond

From first light to pub-time
always the trackless children
skirmishing, sliding
through the grit of empty underpasses;
making a chase game,
throwing Coke-cans, threats,
tumbling down the absurd
grass flanks of the main road.
All day you hear them,
tractors and go-karts squealing
in mindless circles.
All day some are clambering,
stranded on one
rusting climbing-frame.
Others are running away,
and others standing staring
at a vacant play-space.
All through the long summer
they are darkening, hardening
– the out-door children
whose fathers come and leave
in vans or on foot
without a word;
whose mothers are always tired
and shouting from windows.

Making little barbed worlds
from broken glass and match-sticks
at the edges of kerbs,
the children never listen.
They started with clean socks,
new toys, rosy faces,
but always end here
dirty and alone,
one street beyond
justice or love.

Spring

In the ramshackle wood
the stars of anemones go on. How can they
manage such fission, such spillage

of spotless amps on such a ruin?
Even the snow's high tide could not whiten it.
This, this is the place where babies bruise

and good prospects buckle into mud.
A dead Ford, haunches jammed with rust,
sinks sideways, the grass blossoms little papers.

This is the Place, this is the execution.
This is where the red door-mats hang their dust-
mouths on the gallows of black balconies.

This is where the rich focus their hate
of the poor, where dignitaries zoom in on flying visits
to hand out free abortions and bailiffs' writs.

And a yard away from the last
concrete escarpment dwindling to chicken wire,
they plumped under nettles

– frail lights nourished by pram spokes, fired
up the fathoms of dank mud into rubble
and indifference. These children also flourish

on nothing, flushed corollas fat as worlds
in a shrinking space; the same eclipse will break
both brilliancies in no time at all.

The Inheritors

The street lights bronze the pale weatherboard
house-fronts. Beyond their heads, twelve bald
bulbs climb, one behind the other,
up Beech House, beechless as Buchenwald.

Plimsolls pound. A human shadow drops
and coils for cover behind the concrete stair.
The panda car is watching somewhere else.
The broken glass winks under the star.

Outside the fish-shop, knives are flashed.
Down in the play-park, five
girls curse and laugh and jounce the metal horse,
and wait all evening to be snatched alive.

These are the locks they'll wake behind, and these
hard sons the sort they'll struggle not to raise
against the weatherboard and echoing stair,
down the cul-de-sacs as short as days.

Elegy

This is a summer of heat but no light,
the dim gardens uninhabited at dusk
that drifts pale blue and slightly smoke-soiled,
holding little hope of one ripe star.

Only Beech House slowly electrifies
through windows spaced like screens on a light-box module.
If you turned enough dials, would marvellous rainbows flow?
No, they are really yellow room-lights, distant specks

move, eat and die in them.
Generations of lives, they are stockpiled here
or set in rows behind the angular porch-ways
of Foxcombe and Applegarth, the bull-dozed woodlands.

These are the stone fields where the poor are seeded
by random bureaucratic winds.
If they fail to root, there are priests and a welfare service
– no need to cut throats, scream, jump off balconies.

But the summer breeds its own ills. Each night
smashed glass chimes the hour, and wishes bleed
down walls autographed by the nameless young
spilling their small fire into a granite tundra.

Eviction

His wife rising at dawn, rock-brown and wordless;
his knife, African moon-sliver, baring its back-bone;
his dread reaching out into the morning.

The morning, dead-white, simple, terrible morning;
noise of his children, and the pure black baby;
his wife, sugaring whiteness for the feeder.

The jobless years, deserts of unused time;
dead bed where he hunched, trying to smoke out
the dread that always pointed to this morning.

The quick thrill of the door-bell, then the banging,
the tramping into the hall, the thick, flushed faces
of the well-employed, the state assassins.
His wife on the stairs, bringing the filled white feeder.

How he jumped then, apathy behind him,
the years' beached bed-sheets like a sloughed-off skin;
how the knife flexed in his hand. It skimmed her morning

off guard. She swore once, softly. Blood
bulbed like a flower. The children screamed
at a fate worse than bailiffs, their mother dying.

Panic. Panic and power. The slow icing
of two astonished faces. Halted steps.
Sharp as an animal he turned into the bed-room,

saw nothing there to deflect, to pacify;
no trace of pity, all hope soused out
in light and screams and a sheaf of official papers.

He worked decisively in the upstairs room.
The darkness of his children,
tear-brilliant, poured into the open street.

Foot-steps warned. His wife with her torn arm
had snatched the baby, bloodying its cries.
His throat became a mouth, the red tubes falling,

the knife falling, the sun falling. His dread
reached out its claw and fixed each wavering child
to the white vice, the mill-stone of the morning.

Surgery

It's safe here – a square white room
where the air is cooler and the conversation quieter;
where order calmly checks the filing system,

her sensible telephone-voice secreted
behind glass. The roses on the table
unfold from their fresh silks extraordinary happiness.

This is the frail overture to a cure
– Lourdes candle-smoke and the first Aves drifting
like mist above the iron tides of incurables –

and I have merely a hand with a hole in it,
the pus embattling old disasters
in a ring of furious blood. What does it signal?

Outside, where the long road heaps its dead
cell clots of terraces so close they claw
the last blue scrap of space, then turn on each other,

my mind chafed for its inch
for two years, neither winning nor losing.
No blood-stream could bury such a war.

It sobs in my palm. Calmness and turning of pages
will answer. People are human here and bearable.
A web of weariness hangs them close.

– One hope for twenty torn smiles,
they wait to be summoned by the priest of words
with his mind full of reasons and meanings to which there's no ladder

but submission. It will be magic.
He is old and Indian, he gathers fat about him,
and frowns and ponders and accepts a fate he dislikes.

He takes my hand, becoming resolute.
I can bear any pain now; I am loved enough
to survive. Chastened by swab and needle,

all I can do is sit out my cure.
Somewhere there's tension still, eyes trying to stare
through walls. They see a strange girl in bright colours

— but inside me the griefs lie stripped of fever.
Normality is beautiful, a smooth path.
Will it carry me safely from this confessional,

between the accusing eyes with an easy smile,
and into the street where a hard light
guns down the sick and arms the healthy?

I creep to my territory of dull grassed squares
— six gardens bright with women and sun-burned children
who wait for me and my cured self, indifferent.

A Future

The lights of the estate blink on at dusk
– little well-drilled municipals, one for each

porch. Through curtained panes, block after block,
the violet shadows flash

animus of some small-screen homicide.
Out in the real night, bottles are cracked

for real fights, real wounds. I can't escape;
nor can my children, making what the world

would call an ignominious beginning,
their landscape crowded, graceless and cut-price.

Fingers in mouths, they sleep beyond despair.
Toys colour at dawn. A new snow spills

its innocent stars over the pointed hoods
of anoraks shoving into the main street where

plate-glass defines the limits of free will.
Sweets for the unsweet. I take and share

the sugar gems, souring my children's teeth
in lieu of their inheritance. I weep.

Though no-one's starving, and the poorest will
receive his little spring

by courtesy of the state and Montessori
– paints and clay, milk and imagination –

the land-lord holds the clock's trump card. These hopes
he'll blot, despite all miracles but money,

and money he'll withhold against all odds.
The rooms are shrinking fast, the colours die.

With snow-clogged boots the bailiff wanders in,
talks to the baby, comments on the cold,

sneering, apologetic. It is fate.
The price-tagged dreams fall to the darkening street.

Survival

It is my second summer here. A flat dread
sits out each afternoon. I keep my head
trying to work off the dense, inflated, blue
nightmare of half-a-dozen paddling pools,
with my dust-brush and sink of dust-coloured clothes.
The garden's sand and stones where nothing grows
but a shaggy skull of grass; my neighbour's gnomes,
planed off by four low fences, mark the place
where civilisation clinches this disgrace.
Last summer, though, was worse. I slept
whenever the children slept, but couldn't get up,
and didn't comb my hair for a month.
Time swept that stranded death to colder nights;
I tied great Christmas stars around the light
– purple, green, blue, gold – and thought I'd learnt
how to survive.

            Will this summer's dragging hurt
let me survive the lesson? I must hold
with all my muscles the summer's blue and gold.

Magnificat

Snow-heaps cloud our glass-panelled door
with white. On stereo,
the clear D major of 'et exultavit'
branches and flows, is happiness without question
that finds in itself, at length, a sharp enigma.
And abruptly, without trace,
the angel who danced between the casual ear
and the travelling stylus, has flown
from the dust-collecting voice embalmed in its groove.
Not even the first sun-shaft, the D major
commonplace, could hold him;
but somewhere beyond this door, this garden of glitters,
in the flat wastes where vandals
have uprooted the telephone, twisted
the swings into child-scorning ideogrammes,
and smashed the roundabout from its
insubstantial dais
and iron hub small as a prayer-wheel,
his echoes brush reality.
Such acts are as harsh, as surprising
as the rape of the little Jewess
who can't have wanted to be anyone's vessel
so early in her day.
They hurt and illuminate
like a change of key, the dark question-mark
of the interrupted cadence.
The snow cannot hide them with its ordinariness,
but only lies back and stares. Hating such mischief,
the houses, spaced like primary triads,
push their chorales to the sky, but get nowhere.

Ecology

Betrayal

The suburb climbs the hill. Like an eclipse,
its shadow falls across the broken wall
where the last garden dissipates her red metals
for spring's melting-down to the steam of tarmac.

The orchard trees shake and cower behind
their curtains of cold jewels. I am no sun.
My boots smash their aisles, one more town-planner
to snatch the green fruits and promise them pie-houses.

This death is precise. With one stroke it ignites
the rowan's thin fingers, the hawthorn and the rose
trapped in her arsenal of fertility.
Their fires spring in unison to the sky.

They should be left to question the heart, and die,
these doomed mothers cradling pods of blood.
Why do I need to gather their sorrows home
to be scoured and preserved for a winter of usefulness?

The spiders have hung out their murderous silver
warnings over the graves of old flower-beds
where the great golden-rain, the tiger, crouches.
He is gleaming but hopeless. He waits, but I am gone.

In my suburban kitchen I will shush
the awful riches, split the rose-branch stem,
and delve the peep-holes from the sides of the apples,
and shut their eyelessness with snows of sugar,

while the walls of the garden crumble to the screams
of witches with scarlet dresses and spider hair.
I was their friend once, but I betrayed them.
I have a full larder and two clean children; I am the hungry suburb.

Crossing the Border

The round-scalped Cheviots
retreat into North and South,
gathering sheep-whitened battle-fields
to the blue clouds' rainy neutral.

How their lyrical distances
coarsen when you enter them!
To marry a landscape is hard,
its blemishes enormous

underfoot, as the quick ram
lurches to the summit.
The bloody claws of heather
chain each step to their Flodden.

We brood over lamb-skull, rabbit-pelt
– fresh relics that mark out
the strategy of the latest
territorial argument,

while the flash of an aircraft, trailing
through silence its long abuse,
recollects a cruder armoury
that poured from the hills, ablaze

with the gargantuan love of rivals.
On moss-soaked Humble-down
they resolved their differences.
Time and geography

have trodden the two nations
into one rough grave
here, where the gale skims
the border fence, and we celebrate

with biscuits and burn-water.
The small barbs have nothing to guard
but a dark sea of peat-rigs
where the fir-babies stiffen.

They promise devouring maturity
– a rank, black night of needles
that the spryest foot-soldier couldn't
unravel. But, in twenty years,

the forester's saw will have carved
an acre of ruin over the dirt-tracked hill,
its shape slowly returning,
and the small brown deer in exile.

Catholic Childhood

Remembering Morning Prayers

Salve Regina; in honour of your feast
we'll etch our knees with wood-grain, red and white,
– cricks in the back and indifference in the soul.
Will she, the pasteboard queen, attend our sighs,

as, blue on blue, the sulking armies drop
like thunder-claps, worn sandals tipped in pairs?
My eyes grip hard her mortal surfaces,
or close on venial thoughts. Her mysteries

lie somewhere else, the points of seven swords,
the angel's stance, the lightning, the dismay
glowing through dark like fierce high-altar jewels,
plucking the retina with fires of truth.

Alone, I saw her tears and felt the quake
of innocent blood out of the torn heart
– but here, even the martyrs yawn. Beneath
the shoals of virgin coughs I drift awake.

Poor, faceless mother, voice a patter of beads,
form lashed to rocks and walls, helplessly bent
to those who drown, these pious headaches slip
through history now. What blessings came, are spent.

At Puberty

After rain
a blue light settled over the convent arches;

the naked asphalt astonished itself with diamonds;
even the washed-out plaster virgin
in the Bernadette Grotto, and the mulberry tree
propped up and barren of silk-worms,
stepped cleanly out of their decay.

From the back of the music lesson
a girl stared through a window
watching beam upon beam of realisation
incise the long mists of her childhood.

Her thirteenth spring
was born among the tattered pages
of the Older Children's Song Book.

Komme liebe Mai

sang the class, uneasily.
A new emotion,
innocent, classical,
yet making her shake and burn,
was softly unravelled
by the clear-eyed woman who sat
at the black Bosendorffer
with her coquettishness and her merciless
gentle arpeggios.

The elm-leaves turned, silver-backed,
on a wind coarse as hunger,

and nuns in their distant sanctuary,
the dark-blue brides of Christ,
closed their ears to the sin, the soft
tired alto of girls at puberty;
heard still a child's soprano.

O impossible miracles, light
out of straggle-rowed chairs
and school-room floor-boards

– the girl, pale as clouds,
stares for a year, aching
at the vision which has no need
of the speechless peasant,

which will suddenly vanish, leaving
only an enormous grief
like a deep river between them

– the woman who needed nothing,
and the child who promised everything.

Politics

Dilemmas

Blurred news of a war, back-dated missives,
they are posted down throats and into eyes
– a squeak, a flicker, no more.
Like sparrows they vanish everywhere,
their women cloudy blots in the sun's white lens,
the screams of their children a white silence
mottled with too much black
– is it the atrocious burn?
Is it blood or only leaves' shadows?
Is it right or wrong, reason or madness?

Is the camera alive? Can the photographer howl?
Is he too blast-dulled, too harried by his dead-line?
Nervous machine, fumbling for the weak cartridge,
lobotomised computer,
we appreciate your vague and calm pronouncements
a day and oceans later.
As you get out your box of clean bandages
and your bottle of blood, you smile,
'Keep still. I really won't hurt you'.

Meanwhile the planes have fanned out into the deep
shriek of blue above the yellow jungle
where a soldier, one man pissing at a tree,
breaks his own amnesia
with a fart like a sniper's shot,
remembers himself and laughs;
and the luminous axe-headed

vultures shear out of the sun, another death-
fleet to the smoking village.

And, somewhere, mayors in crested Cadillacs
campaign for free buses equipped with showers
and Lily-cup automats, and senators meet
for cocktails, their knife-bright boots
sinking into fine Asian carpet,
closing in heavy ranks like fat black grave-stones:
and somewhere Jane and Anne who are still at school
take the lunch-break to ponder
their wardrobe of possible adulthoods,
fingering the silky plastics, articulating
dismay on dismay.

And, somewhere, the reporter at the phone
places every comma, uses colons
and stops with subtle discrimination;
– they are as potent as words,
and the words are so much lighter
and cleaner and cheaper than their images.
His frown relaxes, he feels soothed
with every sixpenn'orth of syntax he can slide
into the soft mouth-piece, the kind receiver
hooded like a priest in a confessional,
encasing the world in whispers, the wax of forgiveness.

And somewhere, somewhere, somewhere
snapshots of shadows, charred opinions, stories
like bloodied rags of flesh
wrung grey, we've seen thèm all, they clown and crowd
in lower-case, they hang
their placards in the hands that twisted flowers,
and sell new cries to slogan-loving marchers
whose logic is that death is partisan,
whose pacifism flies a secret flag.
Swaying down the cat-walks of self-discovery,
they laugh, they are proud, their passion is comparing
the blisters that burn their feet that do not burn.

Heroes and Villains

The air-raid siren's wail, pitched on its edge
of hysteria, wavering up through tired
valves into the staring seventies, still
un-nerves my parents. It's an old flame
who drags them to their feet, panting a bit,
fills their glasses, remembers names,
while their cold-war sophisticate, their only
surviving child, sits yawning at the heat
of that red sky, fogged behind fumey glasses
where god's Churchillian-jowled above the spires,
where flying bombs silver into
mystic V's, and friends outlast thick fires.
Love fills their eyes. It was a holy war.

My parents, seven years wed
but festive still in silks and fresh khaki,
swanned like liberators through S.E.,
laughing and ducking as the Blitz spat blood-
stars back at them, and missed.
All night while the incendiaries spawned,
they kept awake and close,
crashing each German sky-line to a smoke-
filled void under the white planes of their thighs
– such heat, such vehemence – and still
Auschwitz an un-named drumming in the belly;
Auschwitz a mumbled word for a private deed,
dumb and vague as the old error which stopped
the dark clock of my mother's monthly flood.

All that summer the Blenheim dragon pumped
the home-fires' heat to fever. I uncurled
my ear under the taut paunch where my mother
cast on new wool for her victory December
but no sound reached me. Five years on I probed
the tobacco tin my father'd saved
for one bright button, Royal Artillery,
flame-winged, more bird than bomb, and felt my dreams
thunder with disappointment. Twenty more
years, and I see all life slump valueless;
– my father, blonde and young in pointed cap,
still holding that child, that flashing of white love,
fists up at the sun, and all the young, blonde, fine-
boned patriots we had never understood
feeding to flames under the same black sun
a million more pale children, one by one.

The Making of the Dictator

The hungry pressmen can his mind;
head-lines like jack-pots spill its chat;

the words tickle the voter's dream;
the images nudge the consumer's fat.

The fists shake flame, the mascara winks;
the cameras plant their sparkling shocks,

and still the voter believes his ears
and the satisfied consumer jokes,

'til censors switch the slogans off,
and aides flush out the image – there

the invisible shape forms on the dais,
its shadow taller than the spare

young smiler in the armoured car
that drove across the living-room;

– this sightless eye, mouthed howl, drab hand
in silence draft the laws of doom.

Poem for May Day, 1971

In Moscow, aerobats instead of tanks,
and flaming through Old Town a rampant east
wind. It strafes the bare playing-field
that once was green lake. Two willows still
search the old boundaries for lost glimmers
of themselves, the cinerama of water.
Dark over rooves, the last eye-witness of
still older, witch-ridden marshlands, the Parish Church
booms out tradition on its mechanised chime,
hustling for faith down Bishop-named terraces.
In Church Street traffic scrapes the court-yard where
god's rugged, four-square stance still flags us down,
bells bursting out over our heads
like almond flowers along grey streets; inside
among the drifting whispers no-one prays.
Plaques are read, each altar-piece observed,
while the tableaux in each window still pretend
to filter mysticism from a common light.
The sight-seers leave, shutting the west door
with care. Outside, unseen, the faithful keep
their wooden seats for fate or reformation
– one woman and a dirty child, conceived
each by years of hardship in Old Town,
and the village idiot's latest descendant
nodding his goat-face at an old hallucination.

Scenes from a Legend

FOR P.T.

For each green hero of the latest war
smoothing his battle-dress on a first date with chance
it breathes again, comes like a worm out of time
– the low voice, the tone that always threatened
his traditions of grievance, months of difficult training
– Andromache whispering yes, eyes full of no.
Her nerves bother our radar
far from the wide wall where the fates had thrown
their shadow, cold cloak to Andromache's heart.
Though Hector at her side flashed like a star,
tossed her fat platitudes and consoling slogans,
in the tinsel of sun and cloud above him,
the war-god's shield assembled human faces
– a child's face smashed in blood,
and the bony, well-loved bronze of the Trojan,
his victory glare whitening and fading.

Too soon the real ships, their black turrets
barbing the sky-line, the air becoming thick
with vengeances and ideologies,
stops her heart's shuttle, cuts the taut thread of her sighs.
Once she begged Hector to keep the war low-heat
and local, scarcely caring
whether it was for a god or for a woman,
clan or civilisation,
he put on the heavy glitters of defence.

Now all her instinct cries
that nothing, nothing merits the slow infection
of one heroic mind
with the first bite of its bayonet, not all
the myths of the rulers, the dreams of the common soldier
where justice and dead girl-friends smile again,
worth one closed eye of this
small child hurled by the gilded lords
of democracy against their city wall.

Andromache the little-spirited,
who wanted only her love-nest, husband, wife
and child, too simple even
for the simple politics of bomb and gun,
tumbles the false logic of centuries.
Through ruined front-lines into the voiceless cities
and colourless fields of the enemy
turning the smoking tip
of each spent war-head, she
hunts for maimed demons, burnt-out plagues, but finds
only the lanced individual smile
of another Hector, another Andromache,
a child's dead kitten, a broken dish of cries.

What does she leave behind
in the old country, in the windowless house
but rats, blown lights

and a torn-open telegram
that names her husband, the luckless officer
whose fluent limbs and brilliant strategies
won't even make a pyre, they're so damped down
with disillusionment, so common and small
in such massed warfare? Quiet now, empty-eyed,
she wanders the frozen truce of years,
yet always finally arrives
for smiling drinks in the elegant apartment
of her sensible remarriage. The days are warm,
Utopian the lives of the sallow strangers
with broad skulls who walk about outside.
The old griefs barely stir
her immaculate exile,
its furnishings of well-adjusted hope.
Only her eyes mirror the dead. Their fixed
vengeance waits for her
and all her neighbourhood. They nourish old scores
deeper and blacker than the midnights where
between her insensible thighs
she calls the conqueror home to his hot lair.

Colour Supplement

Congratulations

Primrose 2000 calling for two shy minutes
– Auntie Angie offers you a rave-up in her fourth floor
brown lino city.

Moon-finned Fiat skims beneath her window,
flashing some jumpy queen into her
first major scene.

To-night, eighteen mirrors will lie to her gently
– St Angie of the Empties, eyes brightly shining,
breasts wearing glasses,

and eighteen years come to congratulate her,
smile, fetch her a soft drink and
promise to ring her.

Aesthetics

Caught off-guard by the impudent Laser beam,
alienated by a delicate whim,
the new aesthetes excitedly prospect
with guide-book and credit-card the age of steam.

It is September. On warm holidays
when the West End flickers into humanity,
pre-Raphaelite silks float sandalled feet,
and the subways speed enlightened coteries

seeking the dim hives of market stalls
where a Renaissance glory emanates
from the bland patina of Victorian industry
– daguerreotype, ivory, willow-pattern plate.

Meanwhile the 'Mystic Orient' sustains
Victorian travellers' tales. Its trinkets tipped
onto white cloth by a staring Tamil sell
competitively to the Sadhus of S.E.6.

And the great Hampstead violinist pays
his private Guru, forgotten in Bombay.
Obsessed, they shape the lineaments of world peace
through many a 'finely-imagined phrase'.

Now Blackhill Enterprises close the last
festival marquee. The butterfly falls.
Though money sets ideals in perfect glaze
and transcribes the glamour of old movie stars

into a not-quite-accurate verbatim,
the microbe of death navigates deeper mud
than the epidermis. Science hangs her head
when the beautiful die; she can only donate a post mortem.

Me-Time

Been interviewing my latest grin all day,
but still smell daisy-fresh – a nice, tall boy

in a roll-neck shirt, John Stephen's aubergine,
who watches on the monitor again

that grin flashing through legends of trendiness.
Wheels spin, there's a girl in my Lotus, the smile speeds west,

swerves, brakes, and now it's on my face.
Somebody coughs. Relax. They love to hate.

All things bright and beautiful are fake
and that means me. Just hear those punch-lines make

the laughter-scene. Style mod, intentions trad
– that's what they dig. I pray. Calm down. A hand,

folks, cos I'm proud to have for our next guest
a movie-star who's quit the Wild West

for Vietnam. What's his name? O yes. Hi there,
James Henry. Tell us, what's it like, this war?

Uh huh. The hawks wear doves now? Want to win
only to pack up fighting and go home?

That's great news. Great. The loud-mouth's over-run.
No kid? That's great. Where did I put my pun?

Well thanks a lot for talking. That was great.
I'm sorry. Once again our time's run out.

I'm sweating. That's his best Vietnam thumbs-up.
'You're a pro,' he says. I am? 'I wish you luck.'

The Star is Dead.
Long Live the Superstar

The gods have bounced around the world,
jet-plane to Rolls and up again.

Now they've dropped at your feet, give them a big hand.
Who needs Jesus, who needs the King of the Ravers,

who needs Krishna, who needs Lucifer,
Dionysius, Moses, the Kamikazi?

These four make enough noise for the lot of them.
They are sprawling in the air,

nevertheless, pretending to be crucified,
the strobes pitching great shadows of stained glass

over the taut white faces.
Yes, this is the old religion, good as new,

and offering a million electronic miracles,
the snapped string a sacred sign,

the wild dances a raising of the lame.
The roadies may sweat, scurrying between wires

to soothe and adjust currents as high-strung
as their idols' souls, but the little girls

never get tired. They are burning
everlastingly. Their hair whirls like fan-wheels.

Meanwhile, the drummer is attacking himself,
attacking and attacking.

The battered molecules, trying frantically
to recover their shape, must see that he's obsessed,

his blood torrential, his stance impossible.
On the backs of cymbals, snares, octaplus tom-toms

he rides through the hammer and stirrup of his nightmare,
and is hurled among showers of disintegrating tin

into a dud trip called reality.
Death fixes him, white-eyed, from the bedside glass,

but the fiery acolytes keep dancing;
they shake the drops from their eyes and understand

that even before the first fat flame has licked
the box and its flower-load, a smiling resurrection

will be at the vacant drum-kit, announcing itself.
The star is dead. Long live the superstar.

Local Boy Makes Good

Justin, Prince of Poplar,
the fantasist in the fruit-salad shirt,
a destiny on his mind,
and the Cotton Street washing-girl
he lived with a year
still in there watering
the floor he shouldn't have stepped on
with his dirty dreams
big as fruit machines,
and his disgust;
Justin of the docklands,
boarding a sun-bound bus,
taking off from Blackwater Basin, the cranes,
tenements and masts
reeling like Ferris wheels
as he sweats it out in the cock-pit
of his jet-set acumen, schooled
never to look down
into the storms of laughter
and the white-faced wind:
Justin Adamant,
lifeman of one mind,
who laughed off every crisis,
having taught himself the simple sum

that in Cotton Street the rats
make love, but in Wassermann's
of W.1 there are
beautiful silk bed-spreads, prices
slashed by more than half.

Maturity

In another time
he'd found gods, he'd found messages
golden in all the corners of his brain.
He could even take on talentless depression,
flood-light it, shape it to stardom.
He was the great director
averting maturity
with an epic of commitments.

He took up his ideals,
his shame and his lack of shame
to cudgel the apathy of an English summer
black as a Saigon winter.
Martyr's blood lay upon everything,
a school-desk or a go-go girl,
her thighs fibrillating revolution.

And still he observes his contemporaries
wearing conviction boldly
in this year's colours.
Hollow-cheeked, Sadhu-haired,
they blaze with the old romanticisms,
but now he sees words that don't fit
the cracks made by their lips

and there's somehow no cause to die
any more, to play at Palach.
He has a girl to scrub the last
protest march from his denims
and a government fittest for cartoonists.
The table-talk of his life

goes on, goes on
– a winter journey into common sense,
its only real events
a wage, a house, a car.
Paying no further mortgage
on distant wars, he scans
from somewhere beyond despair
his elegant career.

Women's Liberation

Ad

Depressed, dispirited,
tired of trying?
Or just plain lazy?
Don't despair!
Now you can make
your own amazing
Krazy Kathy;
all you need
is in this chic
zip-fastenered, jet-propelled,
super de luxe
persona-kit.
Look into it, there's
riches for you.
A genuine girl
from a peel-pack, she'll
rise and shine.
This soufflé-stick
– a quick lick –
will give you her face;
these luminous moons
– pots of paint –
will be eyes, this slick
instant atomiser,
hair, and her mouth
– you can make it
in the wink of a roll-top;

peach, plum or sun-streak
– your favourite tint
in a special-seal finish
to give kisses that shine
and words that spin.
The body is easy
– allure from a tube –
just pierce and squeeze,
and there you have it,
the curves of your choice,
the tan and the little
sun-gilded hairs
all down the thigh.
Beautiful animal!
Catch your breath;
there is nothing more;
no Maidenform,
no little X-tra.
All you need now
is to dare
to speak to her.
The words, you'll find,
are everywhere.
Just read what you see,
and await your prize.
Radiant, smiling,
she will rise up,

reach out her arms
and clasp you tight,
radiant, smiling,
and you will freeze
as she starts to devour you
like perfect peas.

The Girl and the Thing God

Shining plate-glass crammed with clocks and faces staring at clocks, Saturday being dedicated to the multi-media, many-faced, million-armed Thing God,

the girl passes gracefully the south-west window of W. H. Samuel, seeking discovery of the self on this consumer sabbath in this mirror of religious manifestations. Her reflection moves like the ghost of an ad-girl struggling for form and substance in the brassy shrieking forest of live time

its tall clocks fat clocks mod clocks trad clocks clocks with revolving golden testicles Disneyland clocks travelling clocks shocking pink alarm clocks clocks with black faces stainless steel clocks digital clocks spherical clocks sunflower clocks cuckoo clocks

all variously shelfed and priced, all arms at various akimbo. A chaos of times that does not, unhappily, equal timelessness, a terrible multiplicity of inaudible, mixed-up criss-cross times chewing rapaciously at the girl's twenty-five-pound, all-wool, boutique-styled, sixty inches of paradise-green self-esteem. Her great mossy tree-trunk of a coat flickers among burning questions

     – am I pretty

     lean enough

     and not too mass-produced looking

for the twenty-eighth day of november in the twenty-first decade of the century of the many-armed, golden, atomic Thing God?

How his pendulums sway, how his fly-wheels sing. He is bright bright brighter than girls' mere bodies, brighter than their mouths nervously laughing, their voices lamenting, their minds dimly intuiting the disastrousness of too little money or too much fat. He has ground to the gold ashiness of a museum head-dress Helen, Simaetha, Garbo, the Virgin Mother, Great Aunt Violet – their inimitable myths. From now on all shall be beautiful, he decrees, for the price of beautiful clothes and expensive cosmetics – sauna baths, kohl and the labour of manicurists, nylon, sealskin and proteins in bottles. But the palace of the Thing God is the shortness of time, his armies are minutes and seconds who pour endlessly into the town on horses black as funerals. And he has decreed that no person nor thing, however beautiful, shall remain so for longer than the distance between a scrawled short-hand burble of epithets and its eventual eighteen-point by-line on Vogue super-gloss

savagely scanned even by the girl who pushes home her pramful, and with worn heels shatters the puddles, and thinks seriously of suicide

on this star-studded, jostling, note-rustling Film Première of a Consumer Sabbath.

And, all over the town, infinitely glittering windows cloud with the curvings of breasts and thighs, the shadows of brown, grey, white and scarlet skirts and bodices, the wrinkled ankles of boots, the sharp eyes and pale, peaking lips questioning prayerfully the moon faces and numerously pointing hands of the great Thing God

– is this our moment, our orgasm, saint-hood at last?

or even at the high noon of our festival spend-out are we

still overtaken

    worn-dated

by some star somewhere with limitless cash and limitless
opportunity, who queens supernaturally on the crest of each
new minute, the illimitably in, immortally beautiful high
priestess of the church of Things Unlimited?

Even the Thing God pales. What a terrible baby to worship.
Better to crawl home among the middle-aged failures, at one
with every powdered-in wrinkle and slopping-over waist-line,
chained by suspenders and sunken into fur-lined ankle-boots.

Dear God, mouthed the face in the window, let me hate you,
let me detest all images, let me be imageless

    let me be brave enough to let you devour the perfection of
the identikit leaving only the sacred bloody-awfulness of the
identity˙

    eclipse yourselves, galaxies of shining faces

whose lewd mouths open onto my twenty-five-pound sixty-inch
paradise-green sell-out, mocking. Whose steely arms and
glittering sun-heads enclose me with an image at every turn.
Whatever I wear, however plain, square, subversive will cost
too much and smother me in its masks.

Even blue jeans bear complex telegrams.

Even to wear no clothes is to take up a political stand.

The identity is the image, the image is the identity. The
Thing God has eaten the girl long ago.

    under the coat

    there is nothing.

Houses by Day

Houses by day have silent insides;
they are solitude illuminated,
their spiders motionless, their dust intact.

I have lived here an impenetrable year
with only a mirror to smile at and a hot water system
for an echo. I can just remember

an earlier day-light, a taller house
sliced into dank flats, the land-lord always away.
His pinched rooms glowed on our pioneer emotions.

It was the high mid-sixties;
wine bottles hogged the fire-place and lust flamed,
the Beatles louder than the repetitive wall-paper

when I woke in our junk-shop double bed
from a broken dream to an indissoluble law.
The tight ring dragged on my thickening finger.

The trauma of marriage swallowed me. I became
a ghost whose buried rage hoists furniture,
whose stultified self rattles in the attic.

Adjusted now, I have learned my role is to wait
for the key in the lock, to serve the first clean kiss
and light up at a flick of my clitoris.

Ovulen 50

This is a galaxy
— twenty-one bitter stars
in a light-blue disc of space.
Pills that have altered history,

they sit like stoppers
where life would pour out wildly.
They leave nothing to chance.
Their refusal is absolute.

I ask myself how I can continue
night after night to absorb
their tinkering incursions.
They have come not from fields but a brain

playing chess in its sterile factory
with rats and phials.
Now ranged in platoons, they advance
like aliens, offering the world

strange fruits of occupation;
promising the hungry-eyed
women whose only
gift for centuries had been children,

a liberated destiny
among filing cabinets and addressographs.
Attractive, lucrative,
their waist-lines hidden in smocks,

the women fatten industry,
but worry and worry
at a lean obsolescence inside them.
I too lie awake

counting the days
since my womb unsealed its mourning
of red half-hearted flowers.
These chemicals do not love me;

they bring a sickness that's stranger
and far more sick than the early cry
of the stomach envying
a sprouting upstart

rollicking in its downstairs room.
This is the nausea of nothingness
– no travelling egg, no frenzy
in the divided nucleus,

but the slow drip of a carefully-
synthesized hormone-blend.
It smiles as it kills me, and tells me
I'm lucky to have such freedom.